SHE

A GLIMPSE INTO HER INNER TURMOILS

HANNA FATHIMA KHAN

Made with ♥ on the Notion Press Platform
www.notionpress.com

For her.

I know the world was not easy on you darling. Yet you made it this far.
Just remember that I'm so damn proud of you.

Contents

Contents

Contents

The Author

Hanna Fathima Khan, born on 23rd April 2004, is a budding Writer, Poet, and Spoken English Trainer residing in the beautiful lands of Kerala, India. She grew up completing her schooling in Kerala, Tamil Nadu and Karnataka and is currently pursuing BSc Psychology in Al Jamia Arts and Science College, Perinthalmanna. With the continuous shifting of place and getting to know new people, books were her only constant rock and friend throughout. Her love of reading slowing built a spark to write. 'She' and 'Resounding Silence' are her latest poetry books after a break of 3 years. She authored the titles 'Presidents at Quest', 'Backbenchers at Quest', 'The Voyage of my Heart and Soul', and, 'The Walk between Birth and Death'. She hopes to write more in the future.

1. HER LIFE

Life's pretty sad.
For her.
Bottled up emotions,
Revolting feelings,
Untold stories,
Scarring experiences,
Unshed tears,
Aching heart,
All just like the air,
Goes unnoticed, evaporated.
Like the stars,
Fighting its way for years,
To be visible to our eyes, yet,
Yet taken for granted;
Sorrow grew day after day,
Lump after lump,
Spreading like cancer,
Extinguishing every last bit of warmth.
It's really sad.
Her life.

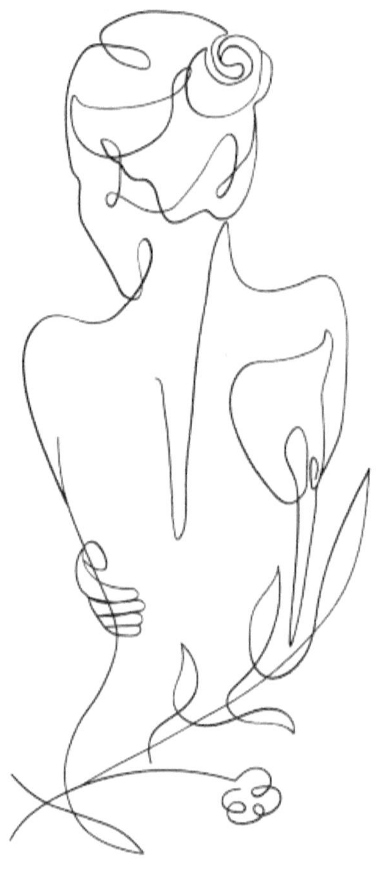

2. HER BURDENS

As time went on,
Her burdens multiplied,
Growing heavier and heavier,
Spreading throughout her.
Until,
Her heart was cold,
Her cheeks pale,
Her eyes lifeless.

3. HER WORDS

And then,
She sat in the silence,
Escaping to a world of her own;
Writing out her story; her life.
Pouring her heart out in her words.
Her words,
Her musings,
Her soft mumblings,
That no one ever listened to.

4. STORM UNCHAINED

As his hands rose,
She cowered to the cornerspace;
As his sound got loud,
She covered her ears in haste.
As he destroyed her life,
She bend down and let him reign;
But as he turned to the kids,
She rose, a storm unchained.

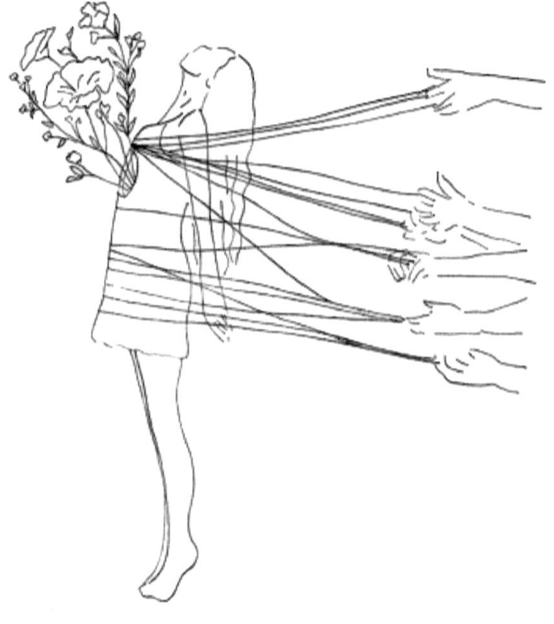

5. BETWEEN DREAMS AND DUTIES

She had the world to conquer,
Her dreams that's her anchor;
But duties, they're to be fulfilled,
Her obligations deeply instilled.
She stands at the crossroads,
Dreams and duties singing odes;
Finding a balance scale,
That'll help her set the sail.
Her dreams were of the stars,
Her duties rose from her scars;
She danced to this song,
Carrying them both along.

6. FIRE WITHIN

She was a storm unchained,
A battle hardly restrained;
A warrior that's strong,
Singing the ultimate song.
She was told to be the flower,
Soft and sweet in every hour;
A doll that's easy to bend,
A weakling for them to defend.
But she was the Knight,
That held her own fight;
A still standing survivor,
A soul burning with fire.

7. A MOLD NOT MINE

She was told to be soft and graceful,
Setting a mold for her to own,
A puppet dancing to their rules.
She was told to immerse in pink,
To love the flowers and the dolls,
A performer, dancing to their song.
She was told to bear children,
To stay home and heed his words,
A slave, offsprings producing machine.

8. YEARNING

She's got a missing part,
Thats hollow and void in her heart;
The world was too cruel from the start,
Treated like a doll for sale in the mart.
She was no one's priority,
Never treated with loyalty;
She felt she was losing her sanity,
From all the insincere amity.
She all her life yearned,
For a bond that can't be burned;
She thought she'd finally learned,
-of betrayal, but was spurned.

9. DEPRIVED

Her well of tears has dried,
Her heart with scars denied,
Her tired soul died,
Her will to live deprived.

10. LOVE THAT IS POETRY

She craves this feeling,
One that keeps her sane;
She finds it truly appealing,
One that numbs her pain.
She wants to be in it,
Fall like the shooting stars,
She wants to be hit,
Fall in the tunes of guitars.
She is waiting in turns,
For her one in symmetry
She really yearns,
For love that is poetry.

11. UNRESTRAINED

She was the fire untamed,
A warrior reclaimed,
The strength, unrestrained.

12. BETWEEN BROKEN PIECES

The branches she'd built of strength,
Wilting, withering, waning and weak;
Helplessness, creeping in stealth,
A moment to breath is all she seek.
And then between her broken pieces,
An olive branch slowly stretched in;
Straightening all her lines of creases,
Calming the brewing storm within.
That short time was all she required,
A moment to be just her inner being;
She's now as resilient as she'd desired,
With a lighter heart; peaceful and freeing.

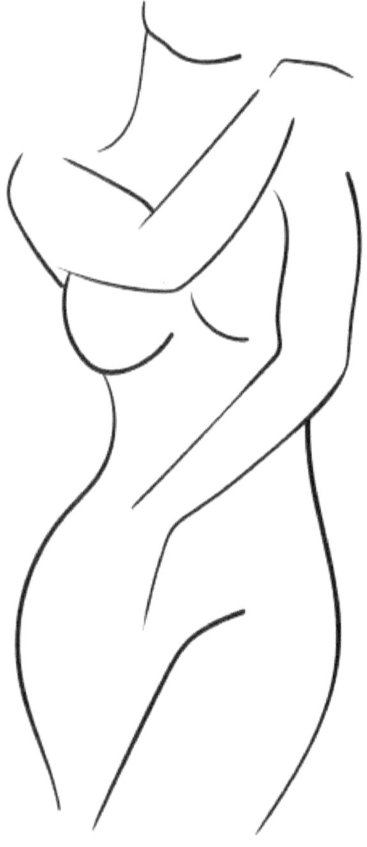

13. EMBRACING THE SHADOWS

She didn't know how much longer
-she could keep the act up.
She didn't know,
Maybe that's why:
She enjoyed the dark,
Maybe thats why;
She found peace in the dark.
For she was herself,
In her realest form;
Among the shadows.

14. MOONLIT SCARS

She adored the moon,
Whispering the tales of hers.
It's craters and rilles,
Mirroring her million scars.
The dark and the night,
Reminding of her void heart.
As it alone stands,
Echoed her lonely life.
The silence that it kept,
The aftermath of the hours she wept.
She adored the moon,
For in it, she found her own.

15. WEIGHT OF AGONY

Life laughed at her misery,
Snatching away all she had;
Cursing her a life of agony,
A spirit in suffocation clad.
She had no girlhood,
Days of laughter, she'd none;
Forever alone she stood,
Shattered remains trying to be one.
Responsibilities followed maturity,
Duties shunning dreams;
None to feel a sense of security,
Her life tearing at the seams.

16. PLANTED

Planted in her womb,
A Heartbeat, the essence of life;
A flower yet to bloom,
A transition to mother from wife.

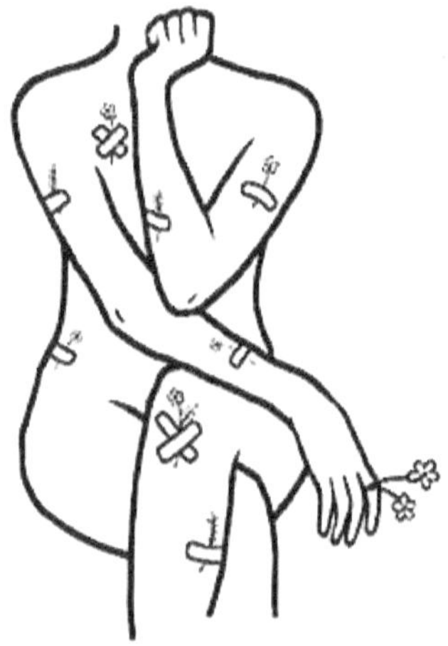

17. FADING

Beaten and broken to nothing,
Shattered remains to pick up;
She was once a surrendered slave,
Hanging on a thread of life.
Counting each day as it pass,
Barely making through nights;
She was once a fading breath,
Wilting beneath the weight of time.

18. THAT KIND OF LOVE

She craves intimacy,
One to hold close and dote;
She desires that kind of love,
That's rare to find or note.
She wants to be a priority,
Among the ones she keeps near;
She desires that kind of love,
That's heartfelt and sincere.
She aches for empathy,
A soul that understands;
She desires that kind of love,
That holds, not just with hands.
She thirsts for devotion,
To trust when others won't;
She desires that kind of love,
That stays when seasons don't.

19. HEART NERVES

The heart nerves breaks,
Every time you're soul's wounded;
Lord, shouldn't she be dead now,
With the amount of nerves broken?

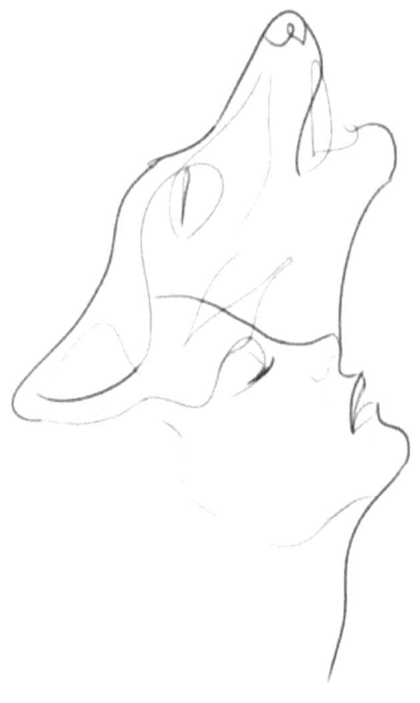

20. LUNA'S ALLEGIANCE

The wolves knew the way,
That led to her heart;
Their fidelity never sway,
Families never apart.
She swore her allegiance,
To the these brave beings;
She admired their resilience,
They aligned her feelings.
To some they maybe monsters,
Beasts ferocious and feral;
For her they were commanders,
Following their Luna's moral.

21. LOST AND TORN

She wandered lifeless,
Lost and torn;
An aching specter,
Her life forlorn.
She stumbled hopeless,
Tired and weak;
A whisper of sorrow,
Sad and bleak.

22. VICIOUS

When everything finally turned right,
Days started looking fun and bright;
Life had to mock her again,
Throwing hurdles, causing pain.
When everything finally clicked,
Fate barged in and luck tricked,
Dreams she built with love and might,
Destroyed again in endless fight.
When the cycle started once more,
Shattering her to the core,
She rose up, even more tenacious,
With life she is going to be vicious.

23. WORDS TO HER

I write this note,
For her that never fell,
It is tough but you ain't soft,
You have got a magical spell.
I write this note,
For her that is strong,
The path is filled with thorns,
It'll lead you to where you belong.
I write this note,
For her who is broken,
You are loved darling,
For you these words are spoken.

24. FEARLESS IN HER SKIN

She's fearless in her skin,
Unapologetically herself;
She doesn't pretend,
Molding into others spheres.
She knows who she is,
The aims of her being,
She's rooted to her truth,
Not damned to others glare.
She's fearless in her skin,
Unapologetically herself;
She doesn't pretend,
Molding into others spheres.
She wills herself to stand tall,
Afraid not of her identity,
She feels no mandate,
To fit into their thought.

25. THE END OF WAR

She was at war with herself,
Doubts clouding her being,
Inner conflicts an imposter,
Settled in her headspace.
She drew more and more outlines,
Of her ever growing fears,
Which to conquer? Whom to seek?
Whispers of failure pulling her down.
She felt herself too small,
Cowering to the cracks and holes,
Her hand shivering with panic,
Her voice cracking with unease.
But every war needs to end,
A side has to surrender, the other win,
This time she lead herself to victory,
A spark of faith her reason of reign.

26. ONLY HER TODAY

She's got only her today,
The past best left forgotten,
Her tomorrow not promised,
The now already fleeting.
She's got only her today,
Living not on others care,
Dancing not on time's decrees,
The now already fleeting.

27. BEYOND THE FACADE

She sees beyond the facade,
She hustles for her parade,
She knows she's adrift,
She can't fit in the shift,
She's realised no one's there,
She'd learnt it from despair.

28. FREE IN MADNESS

She is now a mad woman
So she ain't confined in loneliness.
She is now a deranged muse,
So she ain't jailed in her mindspace.
She is now an untamed soul,
So she ain't pulled by being understood.

29. HOW MANY DEATHS?

How many more deaths
- must she die?
Stabs so cruel etching
- her heart.
Stop this punishment
- in disguise.
End this attacks
- of her mind.
She has lived more endings
- than onsets.
Why does she carry a lot
- yet live so scant.

30. YEARNING

She wills to be valiant,
To come bold and strong across,
She wants to be fearless,
To face the world all alone.
She strives to be steadfast,
To set the pace and the strides,
She thrives to be impervious,
To defend any swords her way.
But she also yearns to be loved,
To be protected and held,
She also aches to be cherished,
To know what it feels like.

31. ARMOR OF SCARS

She is an Armor of Scars,
To the last, a story to tell,
They littered her body like stars,
Each, a testament she carries.
She is an Armor of Scars,
The tales brutal, pain real,
She has found her place in wars,
A rising warrior, finding her place.

32. LOVED, LOST, LIVED

She loved the one,
Who read her like a book,
Memorising all her tales,
Keeping her joyous and blissful.
She lost the one,
Who promised the world,
Betraying her sentiments,
Shattering beyond words.
She lived then won,
"Who" not anymore a voice,
Firm and brave her form,
Broken pieces glued on.

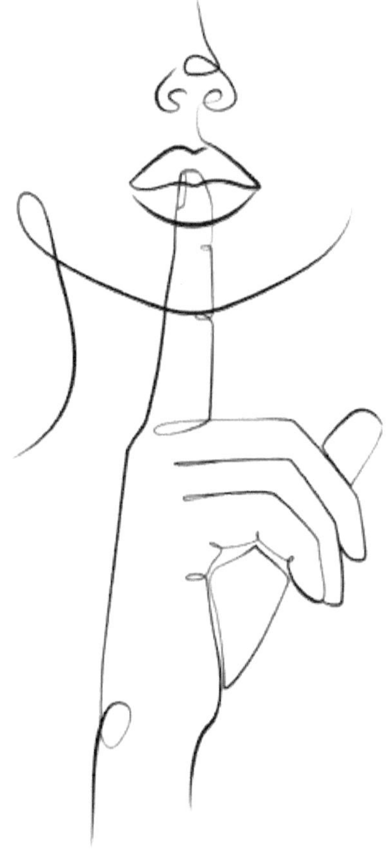

33. LETTERS NEVER SENT

These are the letters,
She never sent,
One of her love,
Other of resentment.
These are the letters,
She never sent,
Writings of her joy,
Anecdotes of sorrow.
These are the letters,
She never sent,
Whispers of the heart,
Secrets of the soul.
These are the letters,
She never sent,
Those who carry,
Her bare souled notes.

34. GIRL IN THE MIRROR

The girl in the mirror,
She looks so worn,
Scars littered her body,
Her eyes, so forlorn.
She's fought against the world,
They kept trying to bring her down,
Every bated breath a waging war,
She feels like she's going to drown.
She looks so unkempt,
A soul on the verge of fatigue,
But she has also got that glint,
Giving up is not her league.

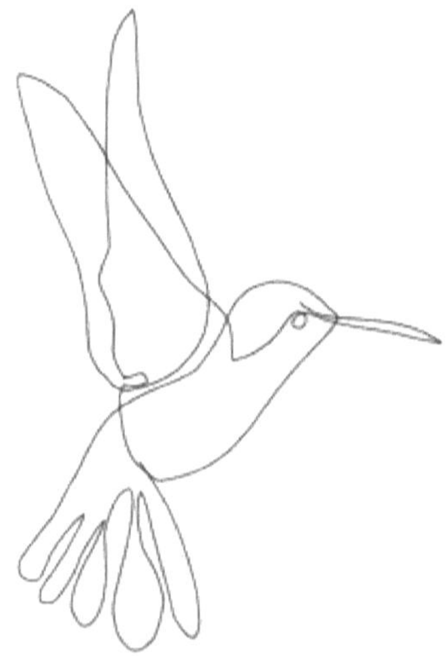

35. LANGUAGE OF FREEDOM

She spoke in whispers, soft yet strong,
Her heart singing a beautiful song;
Her voice, a ray spreading light,
A guidance through the dark night.
She spoke the language, of the unchained,
A final plea, her hopes explained;
Like a river, her soul is wild and free,
She asks the world to let her be.
She spoke the language of Freedom,
One that talks about wisdom,
Exploring the world of insights,
She learnt her inalienable rights.

36. THE WOMAN SHE BECAME

She was once a scared girl,
Her emotions in a whirl;
She was vulnerable and bare,
Her heart in a frenzied stare.
She was new to the world's cruelty,
One that's hidden behind its beauty;
She was pushed into the dark realm,
Her heart learning to be the helm.
Now the woman she became,
A soul that alighted in flame;
The warrior of the dark sphere,
A heart containing no fear.

37. BURIED YESTERDAY

Looking back it's a blood-path,
The thorns peirced her soft feet;
It's a long story, the aftermath,
Fate being cruel in repeat.
Her past is that of tears,
One that hurts the land and sky,
She was scraping off in fears,
She cries to the world asking why.
She has now buried yesterday,
Rebelling for a new start,
She asks destiny not to betray,
The last hope of her heart.

38. SHATTERED, YET WHOLE

She stood in pieces, cracked by time,
Her heart ringing a soft chime;
She was shattered, yet whole,
A poem that has a rhyme.
Her back arched, lodged with arrows,
Her heart yearns to fly with the sparrows,
She was shattered, yet whole,
Emerging from the hidden shadows.

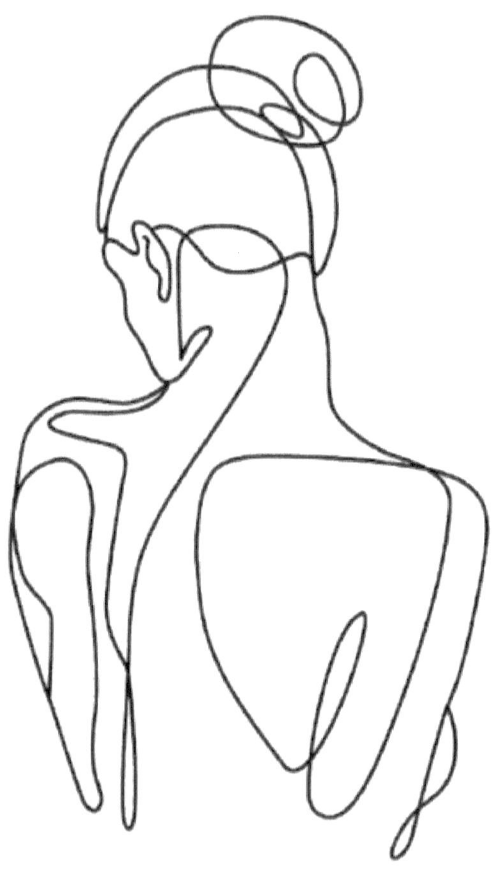

39. HER WRATH WAS POETRY

They called her a burden,
Being born a girl - A Curse,
She was a liability,
In their eyes, even worse.
They said she had a temper,
Throwing fits for petty things,
She was a hot head,
In their thoughts, a nuisance.
But her wrath was poetry,
Born a girl of royalty,
A soul worth fighting for,
She fought for her liberty.

40. THE CROWN SHE WORE

She began at the depths of despair,
Paving her way against their glare,
The path was rocky, the place hell,
In the dirt pit she had to dwell.
Thorns tore her skin, bleeding red,
A wreath of agony gracing her head,
Battle marks adorned her skin,
Every breath taken, a heinous sin.
The crown she wore, an accolade,
The token gifted by the sorrow's blade,
She corrected the crown and stood tall,
Reaching the promised after many falls.

41. UNSEEN LOVE

He was her secret obsession,
This is her hidden confession;
She whispered to him secret tales,
Her life's adventures and all her fails.
She carved his name in all her sighs,
The only solace for all her cries,
He was there but sometimes not,
Never absent in all her thought.
She fell for him, fell for him hard,
He remains oblivious with no regard,
The moon, forever Luna's desire,
But him always in a state of mire.

42. TOO WILD

Her heart -too wild to cage,
Always racing, thundering, pounding;
She had the spirit of the storm,
Fierce, rebellious, untamed.
Her story -too wild to be believed,
Filled with chaos, havoc and mayhem;
Her tales imposible to accept,
But woven with ringing truth.

43. SHE KNEW

She knew there was no one,
Who'll come running to her rescue;
When she's the target of the gun,
Everyone will leave on cue.
She knew there's no tomorrow,
Where everything will be served on plate;
She can't rely on even her shadow,
Or leave it in the hands of fate.
She knew her past's not great,
No joy or things meriting regards;
She began from a horrible state,
Her life in bards and shards.
So she pulled herself up,
Waiting none for one to come;
Overcoming small to big hiccup,
To their rules she won't succumb.

44. LIFE'S CRUEL JOKE

Life played her dirty.
Giving a fake sense of comfort,
To betray her again.
Protecting her from the dangers,
To be the very threat.
Healing her shattered heart,
To tear it apart anew.
Giving her a false embrace,
Playing life's cruel joke.

45. DANCED WITH DESTINY

She danced with destiny,
With struggles no one could see;
Embracing all as it came,
In her heart, an eternal flame.
When things were not so clear,
She never gave space for fear;
The world waited for her to fall,
But she displeased them all.
Destiny didn't hold her in chain,
But was a partner in her pain,
Dance she did with destiny,
Hoping one day she'll be free.

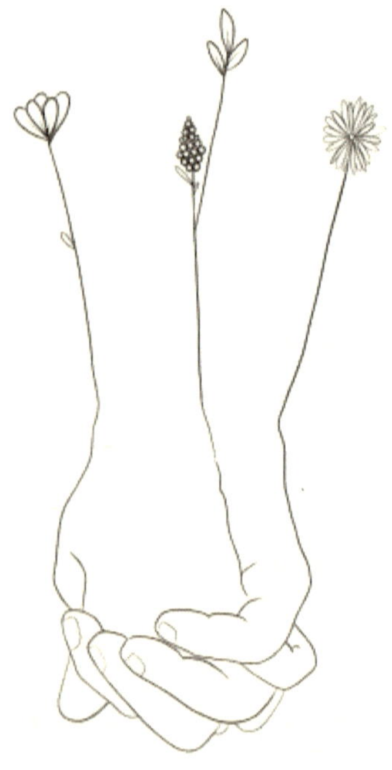

46. LIFE IN RUINS

Her people were her home,
They made her homeless,
Her pals, her refuge,
They made her hopeless.
Her sorrow, enough to destroy the world,
But her heart chose to destroy herself.
Her life now in ruins.

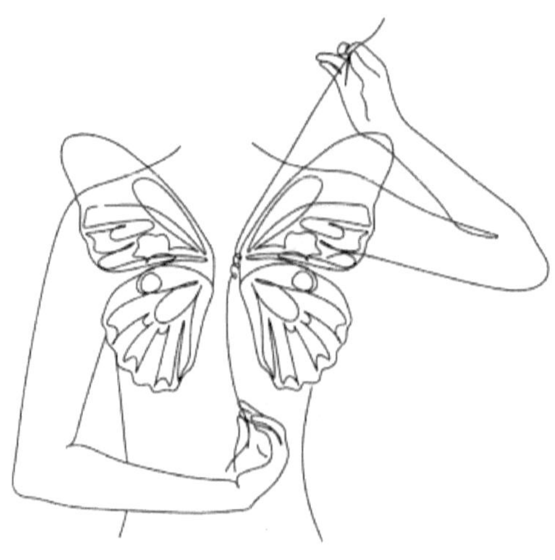

47. POEM SHE NEVER SPOKE

The poem she never spoke,
Hidden in all things broke,
Lost in the whispers and her sighs,
Concealed in all her cries.
It's a silent song in her breath,
A symphony dancing till her death,
The words sealed, a buried art,
It bleeds through the cracks of her heart.
The poem she never dared say,
Lingering in the remnants of day,
Living in her heart that is dead,
One that spreads dread.

48. MIDNIGHT ON HER SKIN

She wore midnight on her skin,
Void filled dark concealing her sin,
Moonlight traced her countless scars,
Countless like the many stars.
She's walked in the darkest paths,
Facing all of the world's wrath,
The midnight held all of her pasts,
Her story that the night casts.

49. LOVE

What's the best revenge?
To love and leave she said.
How to kill oneself?
To love that doesn't requite,
Her voice carrying the lesson
- from past.

50. WALLS BROKEN

She was tough as nails,
A boulder hard to move;
Walking down difficult trails,
She had nothing to prove.
But if someone had opened,
Opened their arms wide for her,
Her walls would have broken,
Seeking the solace that always defer.